100
LEFT HAND
GUITAR
CHORDS

PAURIC MATHER

First Edition - 2016

Revised Editions - 2018 - 2020 - 2023

ISBN-13: 979-8700321303

GTIN-14: 09798700321303

Layout & Design

Hammad Khalid - Malaysia - *HMDPublishing.*COM

Photography

Emma Curtin - Ireland

Translation

Florica Dohan - Ireland

Marco Chu - Australia

Carlos Reyes - Mexico

Andrea Santucci - Italy

InHye Kim - South Korea

Lara von Dehn - Germany

Rafael Mazin Reynoso - USA

Himawari Yamamoto - Japan

Jean-Michel GEORGE - France

Joana Peixoto Meneses - Portugal

MakingGuitarSimple.com

THE ONLY CHORD BOOK YOU NEED

YOU WILL LEARN

- HOW TO READ CHORD BOXES

- HOW TO POSITION YOUR CHORD HAND

- OPEN CHORDS

- BARRE CHORDS

- COLOUR CHORDS

LIVE WEBINAR - VIDEO - EMAIL SUPPORT

For all students learning from Pauric Mather guitar books.
Ask questions about anything you need help with.

Email support@pauricmather.com

CONTENTS

HOW TO READ
CHORD BOXES

Chord boxes are hugely helpful if you're an experienced guitarist. But because they only show you the front of the guitar neck, They do not work for most beginners.

However, if you're a beginner the secret is to combine *"The 3 Step Approach"* (Page 9) with the chord box.

Now they're much easier to follow - and save you time.

T Thumb

1 1st Finger

2 2nd Finger

3 3rd Finger

4 4th Finger

String does
NOT sound

X

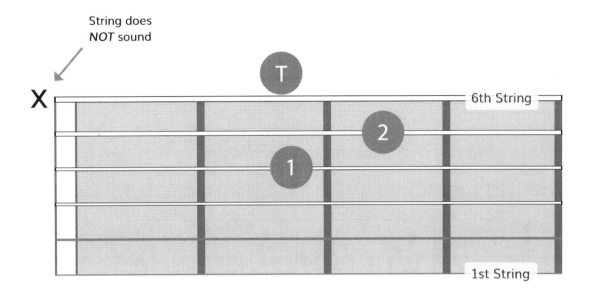

6th String

1st String

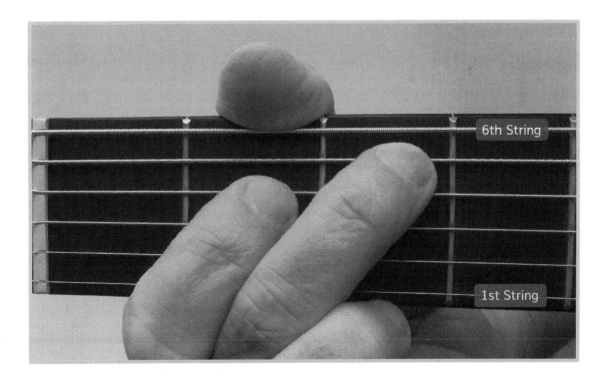

6th String

1st String

HOW TO POSITION YOUR CHORD HAND

Here is the simplest and best way to position your chord hand every time:

1 Tilt your guitar

2 Position your thumb

3 Then position your fingers

This simple approach makes it much easier to learn guitar chords.

And it's easier to speed up your chord changing too, which is the great secret of playing guitar.

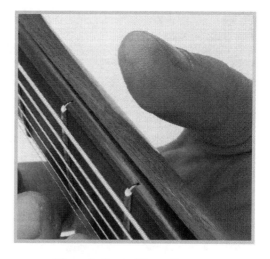

Thumb first - Then fingers

 ## TILT YOUR GUITAR

Tilting makes learning chords so much easier. The guitar is now doing some of the work for you. It also helps to produce a good sound.

POSITION YOUR THUMB

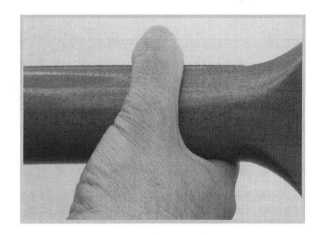

1. Thumb on top for open chords

2. Thumb low and centred for barre chords

POSITION YOUR FINGERS

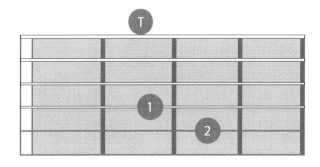

The simple 3 step approach here is technically perfect and exactly as played by top guitarists.

It can help you achieve in weeks, what many people took years to learn.

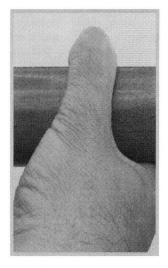  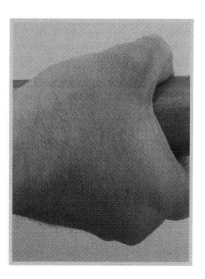

Open chords   Barre chords   Other chords
Thumb on top   Thumb low and centred   Grab the guitar neck

 # THE SECRET

Here is one of the great secrets of playing guitar. In fact without it, nothing is possible.

If you watch any great guitarist, in any style of music, anywhere in the world you'll see *"The Guitar Triangle"*.

- Makes room for fingers to move

- Lets you play with your fingertips

- Prevents knuckles from collapsing

- Makes chord changing easier

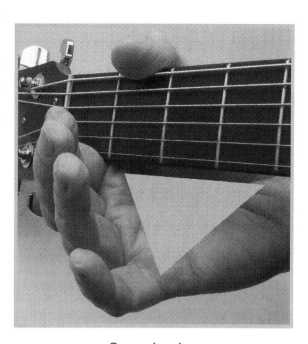

Open chords

100 MOST PLAYED GUITAR CHORDS

A

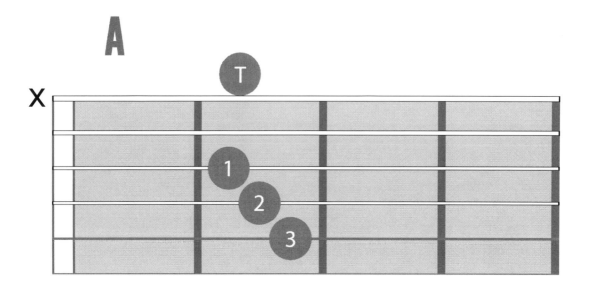

- Thumb touches 6th string
- Squeeze 3 fingers together
- Strum 6 strings - Only 5 sound

A *ANOTHER WAY*

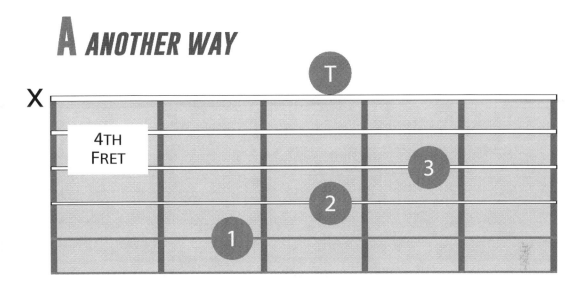

- Thumb touches 6th string
- Ist finger in corner of fret
- Strum 6 strings - Only 5 sound

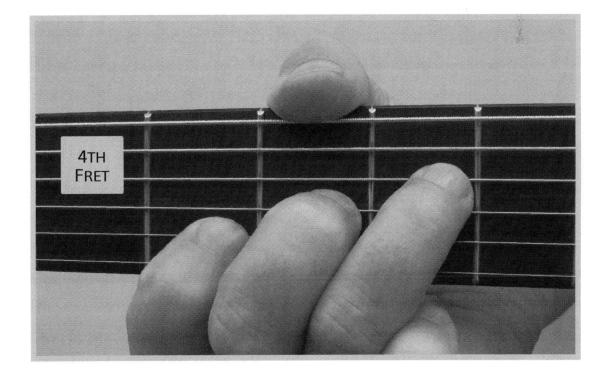

AM

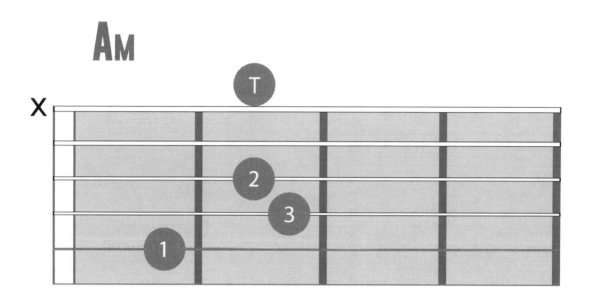

- Thumb touching 6th string
- 1st finger in corner of fret
- Strum 6 strings - Only 5 sound

A/E

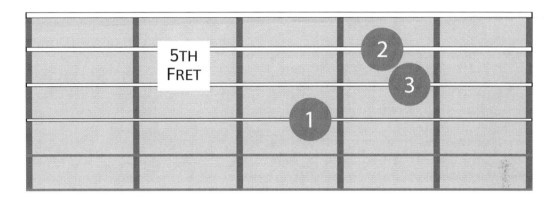

- Sometimes played instead of A
- Thumb not touching 6th string
- All 6 strings sound

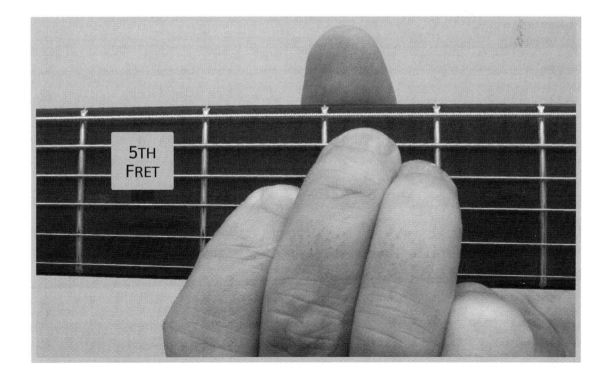

Asus2

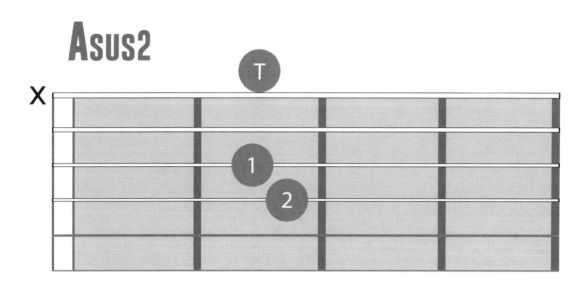

- Thumb touching 6th string
- Can also played with 2nd & 3rd finger
- Strum 6 strings - Only 5 sound

Asus2 *Another Way*

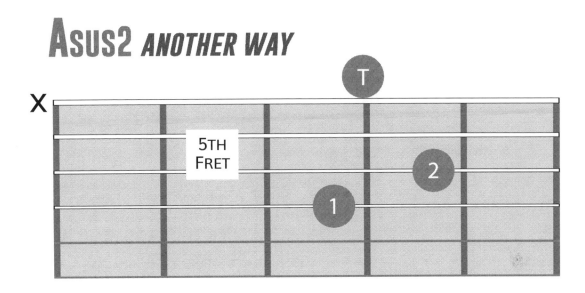

- Sometimes played instead of A
- Can also be played with 2nd and 3rd finger
- Strum 6 strings - Only 5 sound

Asus4

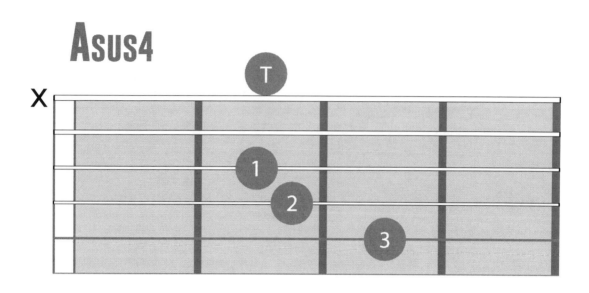

- Thumb touching 6th string
- 3rd finger in middle of fret
- Strum 6 strings - Only 5 sound

A9 sus4

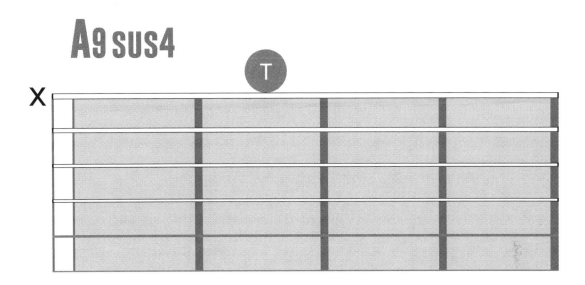

- Thumb touching 6th string
- Strum 6 strings
- Only 5 sound

A7

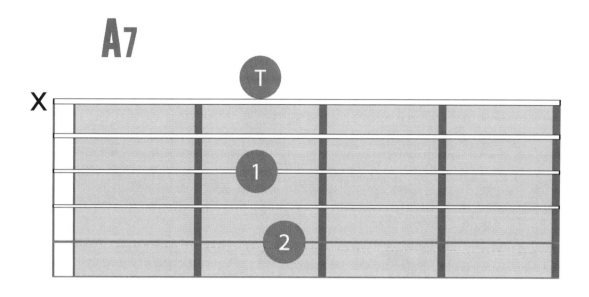

- Thumb touching 6th string
- Can also be played with 1st & 3rd finger
- Strum 6 strings - Only 5 sound

A7sus4

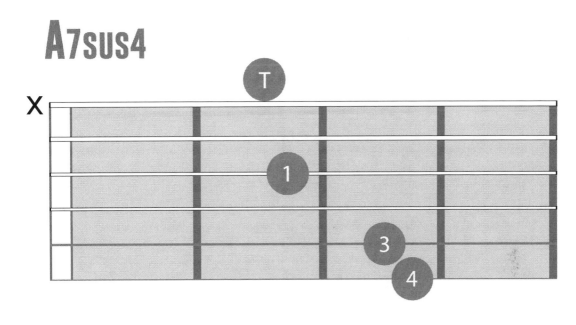

- Thumb touching 6th string
- 3rd finger in middle of fret
- Strum 6 strings - Only 5 sound

A7sus4 *EASIER*

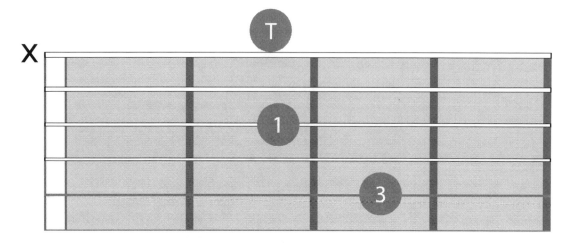

- Thumb touching 6th string
- 3rd finger in middle of fret
- Strum 6 strings - Only 5 sound

A7SUS4 *ANOTHER WAY*

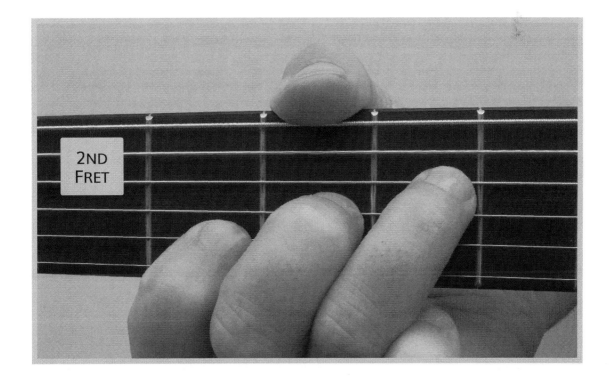

- Sometimes played instead of G
- Thumb touching 6th string
- Strum 6 strings - Only 5 sound

Amaj7

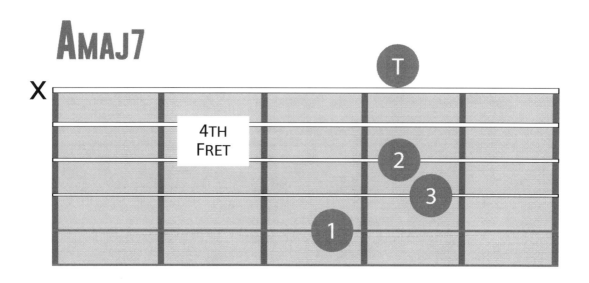

- Sometimes played instead of A
- Thumb touching 6th string
- Strum 6 strings - Only 5 sound

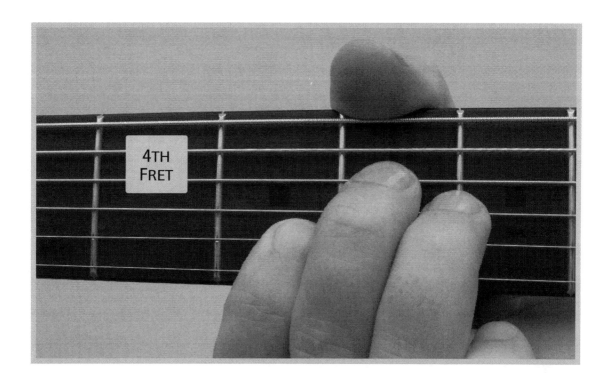

AMAJ7 *ANOTHER WAY*

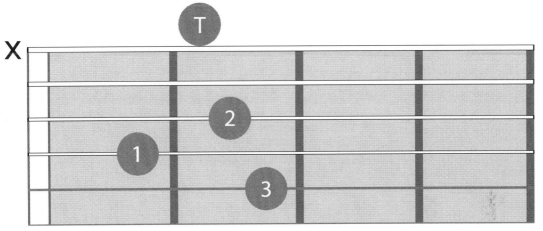

- Thumb touching 6th string
- 1st finger in corner of fret
- Strum 6 strings - Only 5 sound

Am7

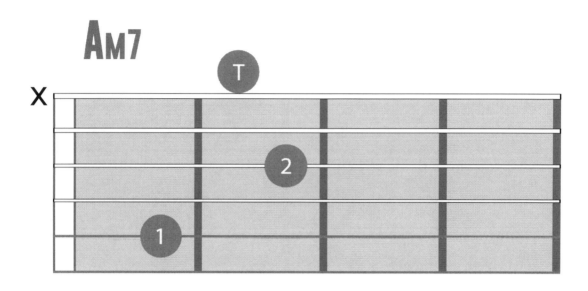

- Thumb touching 6th string
- 1st finger in corner of fret
- Strum 6 strings - Only 5 sound

AM7/G

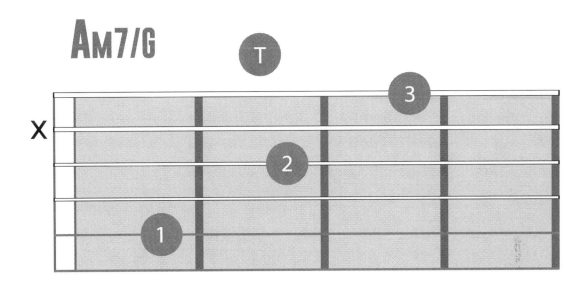

- Thumb not touching 6th string
- 5th string muted by inside of 3rd finger
- Strum 6 strings - Only 5 sound

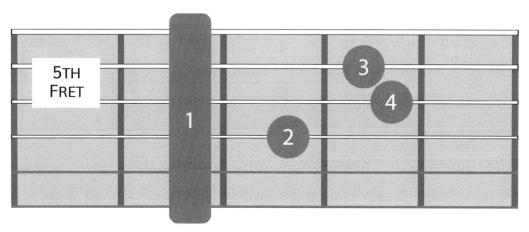

- Stretch your hand
- Thumb low and centred
- All 6 strings sound

B♭M

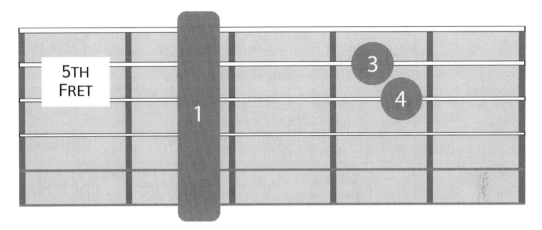

5TH FRET

- Stretch your hand
- Thumb low and centred
- All 6 strings sound

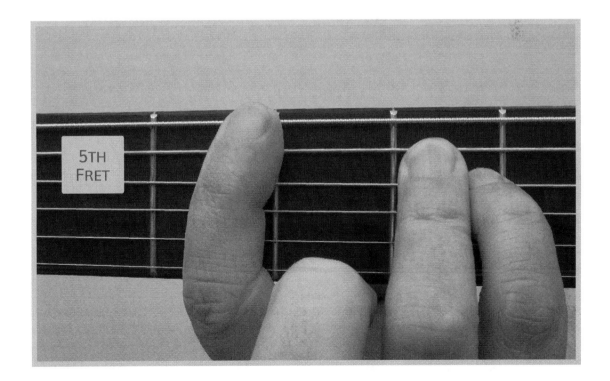

5TH FRET

B♭5

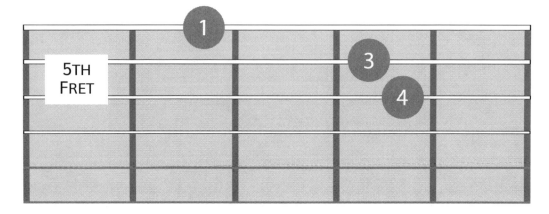

5TH
FRET

- Stretch your hand
- Thumb low and centred
- Strum 6th 5th and 4th strings

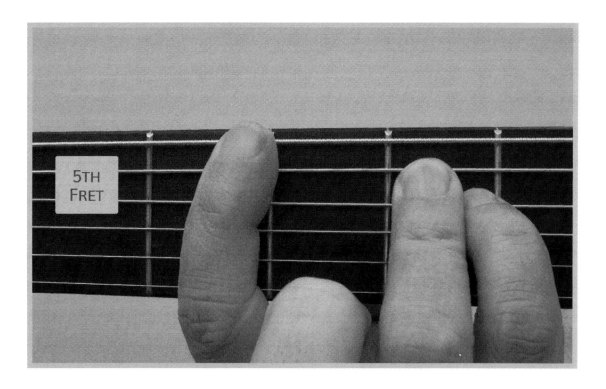

5TH
FRET

B5

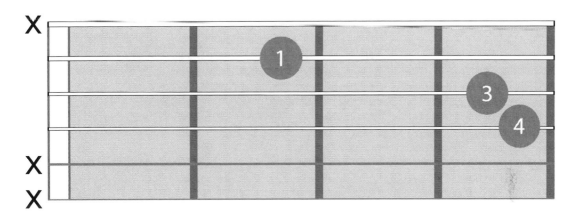

- Thumb low and centred
- 1st finger touching 6th string
- Strum 4 strings - Only 3 sound

B

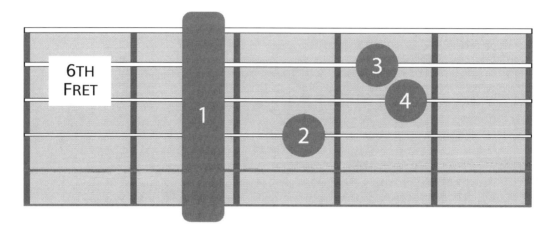

6TH FRET

- Stretch your hand
- Thumb low and centred
- All 6 strings sound

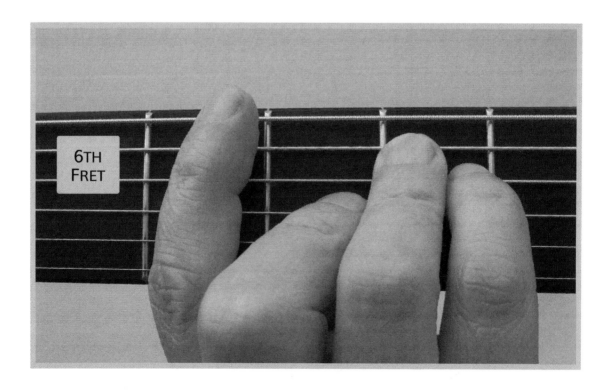

6TH FRET

B EASIER

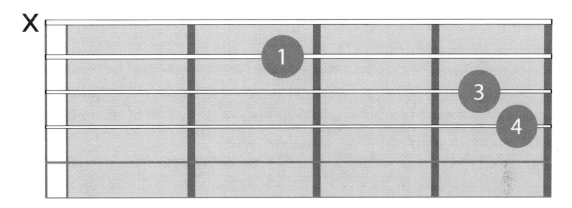

- Thumb low and centred
- 1st finger touching 6th string
- Strum 6 strings - Only 5 sound

Bm

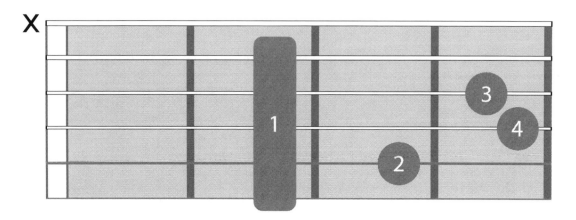

- 1st finger touching 6th string
- Thumb low and centred
- Strum 6 strings - Only 5 sound

Bm *EASIER*

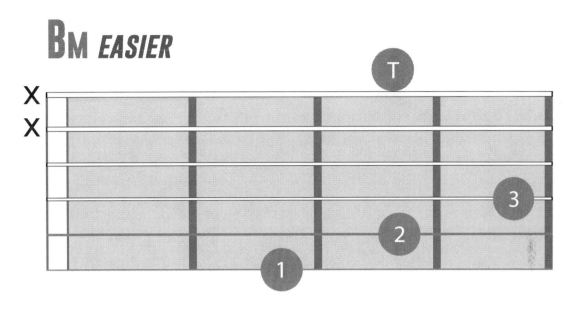

- Thumb touching 6th string
- 1st finger in corner of fret
- Strum bottom 4 strings

Bsus2

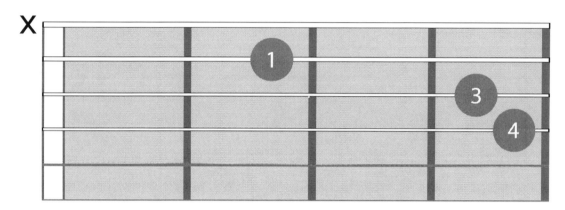

- Sometimes played instead of B
- Thumb low and centred
- Strum 6 strings - Only 5 sound

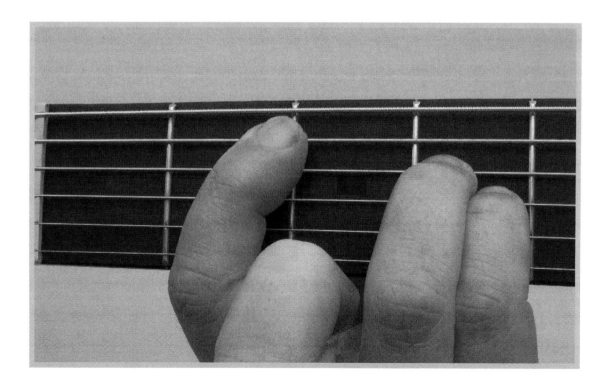

Bsus4

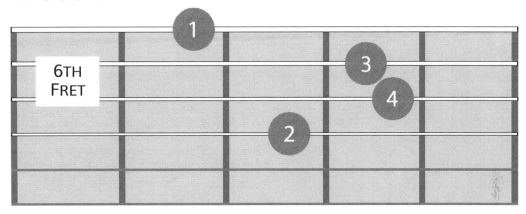

- Sometimes played instead of B
- Thumb low and centred
- All 6 strings sound

B7

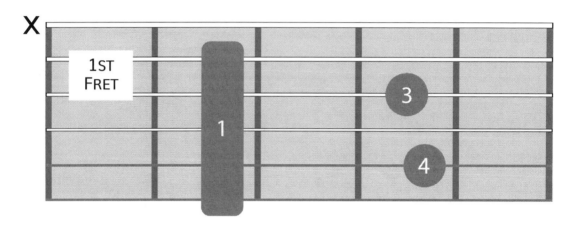

1ST FRET

- Thumb low and centred
- 1st finger touching 6th string
- Strum 6 strings - Only 5 sound

1ST FRET

B7 *EASIER*

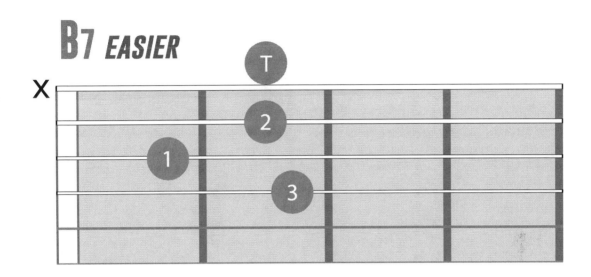

- Thumb touching 6th string
- 1st finger in corner of fret
- Strum 6 strings - Only 5 sound

Bm7

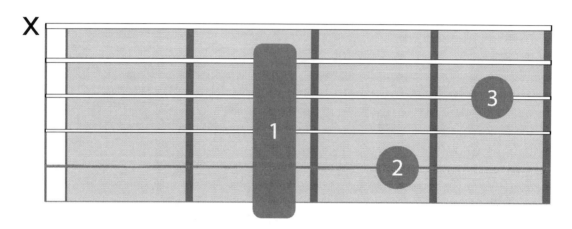

- 1st finger touching 6th string
- Thumb low and centred
- Strum 6 strings - Only 5 sound

Bmaj7

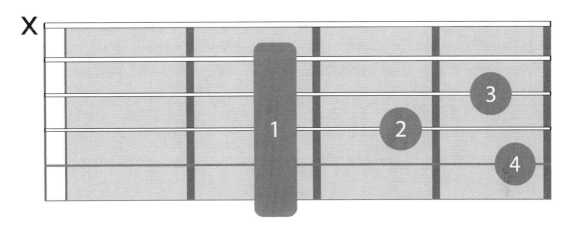

- Thumb low and centred
- 1st finger touching 6th string
- Strum 6 strings - Only 5 sound

Bm11

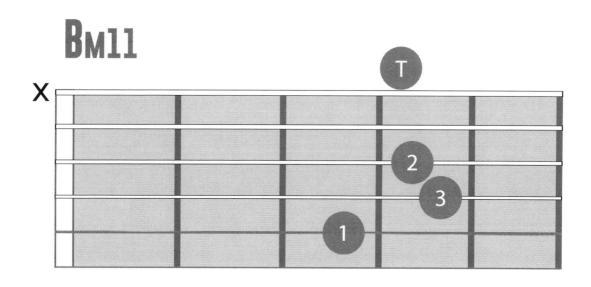

- Sometimes played instead of Bm
- Thumb touching 6th string
- Strum 6 strings - Only 5 sound

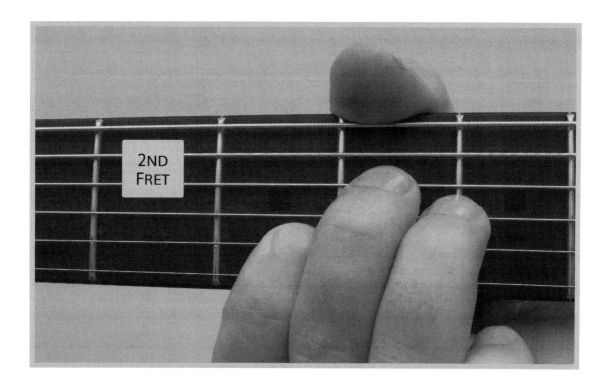

2ND FRET

B/E

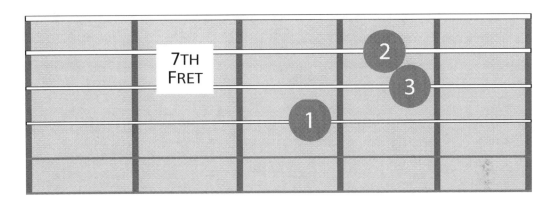

7TH FRET

- Sometimes played instead of B
- Thumb not touching 6th string
- All 6 strings sound

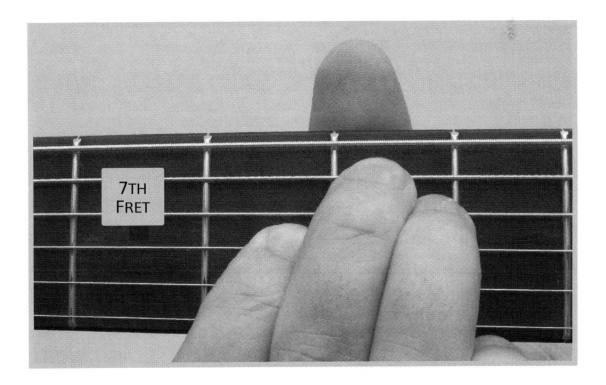

7TH FRET

C

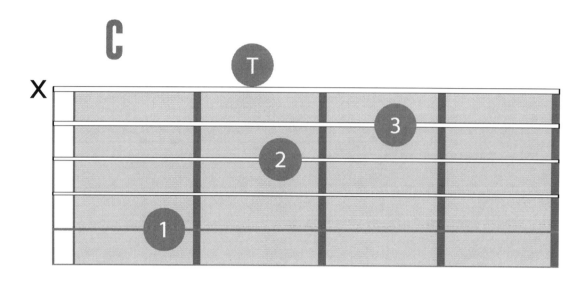

- Thumb touching 6th string
- 1st finger in corner of fret
- Strum 6 strings - Only 5 sound

C *ANOTHER WAY*

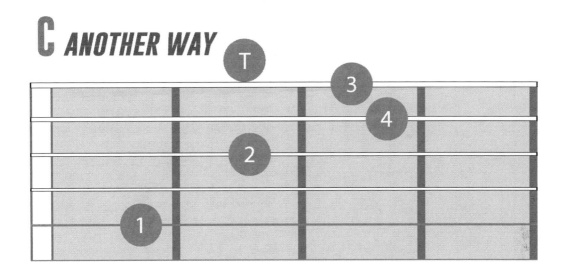

- Thumb touching 6th string
- 1st finger in corner of fret
- All 6 strings sound

Csus4

- Thumb touching 6th string
- 1st finger in corner of fret
- Strum 6 strings - Only 5 sound

C5

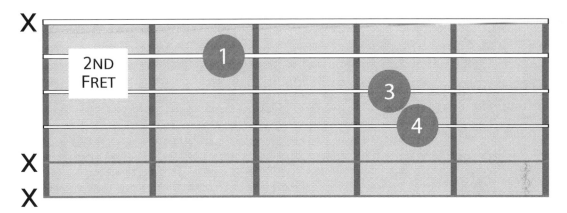

- Thumb low and centred
- 1st finger touching 6th string
- Strum 5th 4th and 3rd strings

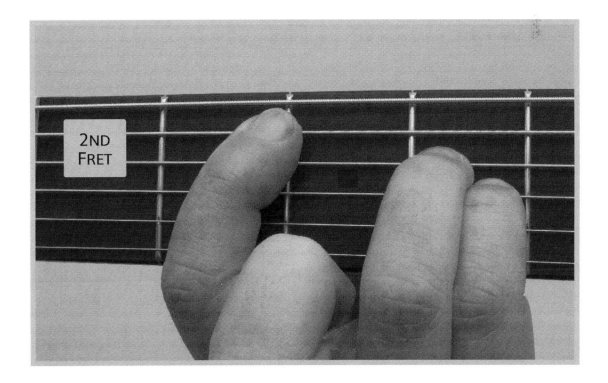

C7

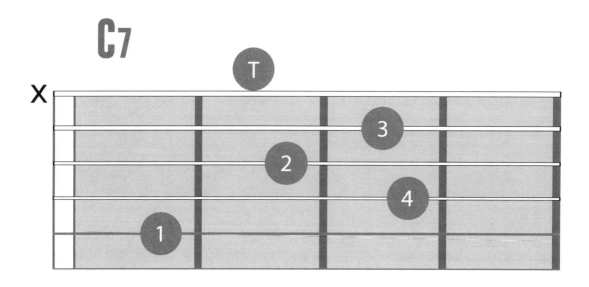

- Thumb touching 6th string
- 1st finger in corner of fret
- Strum 6 strings - Only 5 sound

Cm7

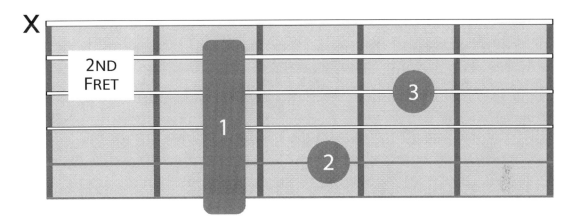

- 1st finger touching 6th string
- Thumb low and centred
- Strum 6 strings - Only 5 sound

CMAJ7

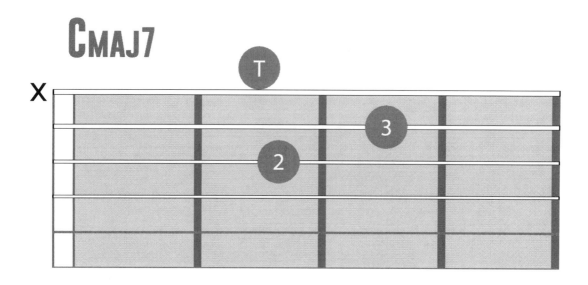

- Thumb touching 6th string
- Can also be played with 1st & 2nd fingers
- Strum 6 strings - Only 5 sound

CMAJ7 *ANOTHER WAY*

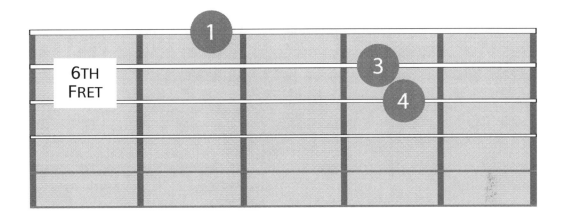

- Stretch your hand
- Thumb low and centred
- All 6 strings sound

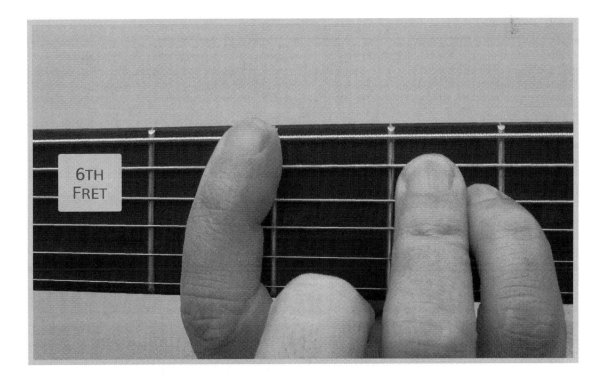

Cadd9

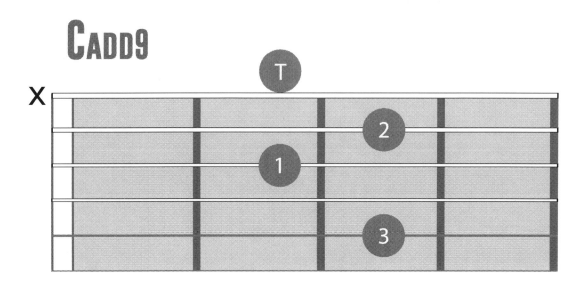

- Sometimes played instead of C
- Thumb touching 6th string
- Strum 6 strings - Only 5 sound

CADD9 *ANOTHER WAY*

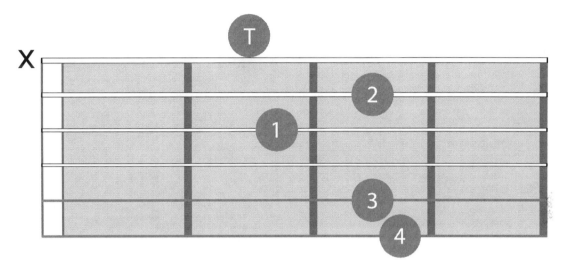

- Thumb touching 6th string
- 3rd finger in middle of fret
- Strum 6 strings - Only 5 sound

C/B

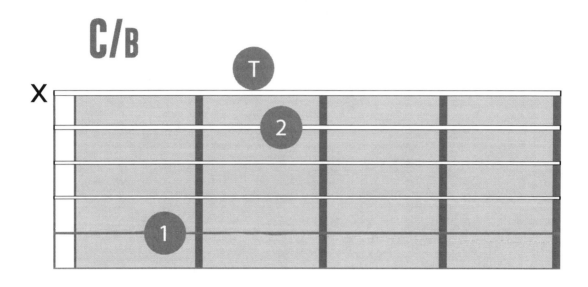

- Thumb touching 6th string
- 1st finger in corner of fret
- Strum 6 strings - Only 5 sound

C/G

- Thumb may or may not touch 6th string
- 5th string muted by inside of 3rd finger
- Strum 6 strings - Only 5 sound

C/E

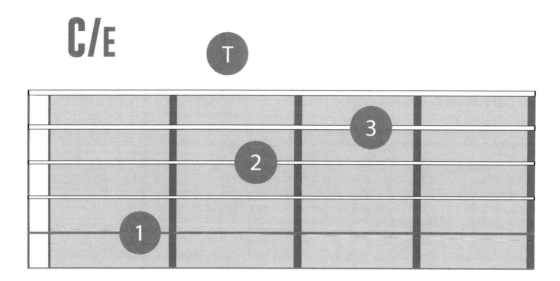

- Thumb not touching 6th string
- 1st finger in corner of fret
- All 6 strings sound

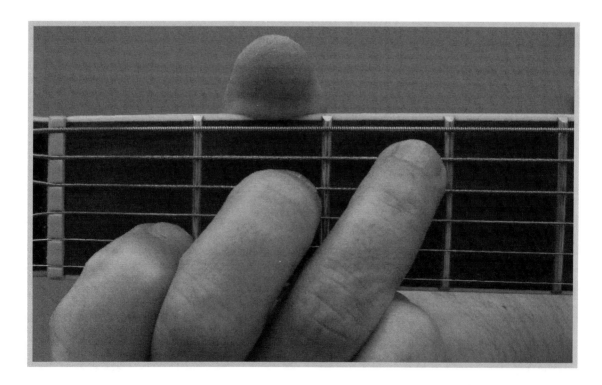

C/E *EASIER*

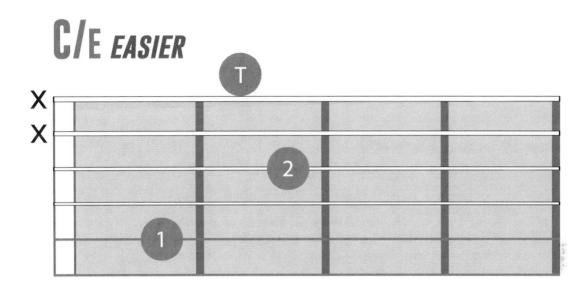

- Thumb touching 6th string
- 1st finger in corner of fret
- Strum bottom 4 strings

C#M

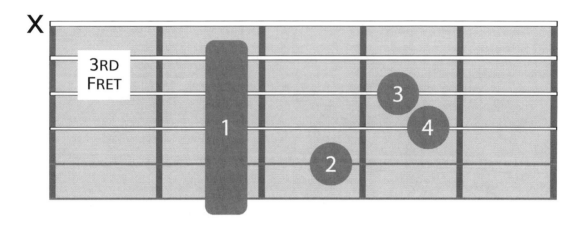

- Thumb low and centred
- 1st finger touching 6th string
- Strum 6 strings - Only 5 sound

C#M *EASIER*

X

3RD
FRET

1

3

4

- Thumb low and centred
- 1st finger touching 6th string
- Strum 6 strings - Only 5 sound

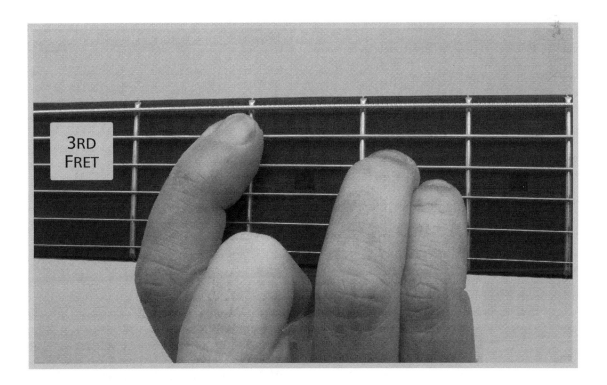

3RD
FRET

C#5

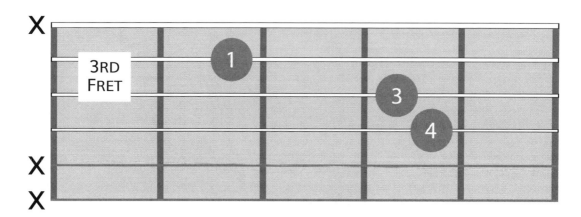

- Thumb low and centred
- 1st finger touching 6th string
- Strum 5th 4th and 3rd strings

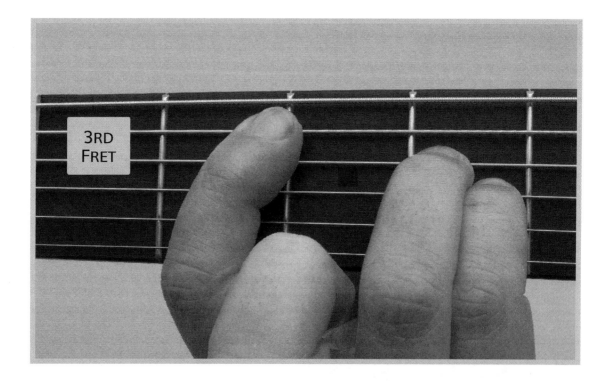

C#M7

X

3RD
FRET

1

3

4

- Sometimes played instead of C#m
- Thumb low and centred
- Strum 6 strings - Only 5 sound

3RD
FRET

D

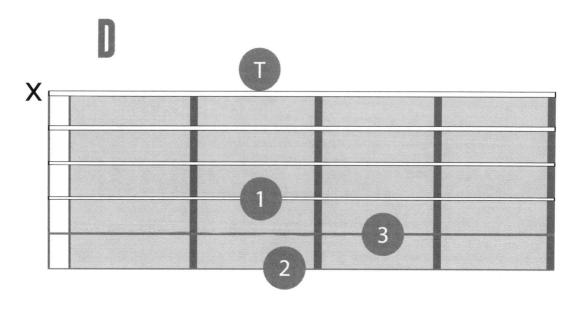

- Thumb touching 6th string
- 3rd finger in middle of fret
- Strum 6 strings - Only 5 sound

D_M

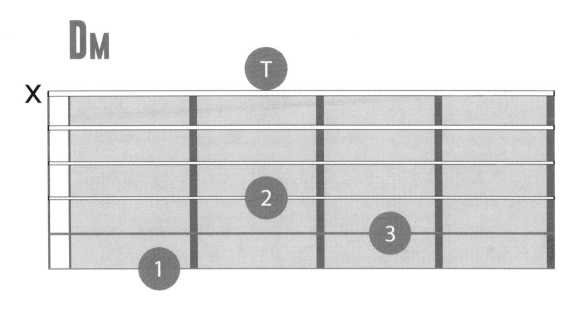

- Thumb touching 6th string
- 3rd finger in middle of fret
- Strum 6 strings - Only 5 sound

D/B

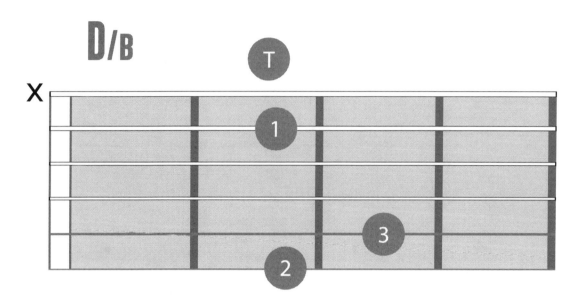

- Thumb may or may not touch 6th string
- 3rd finger in middle of fret
- Strum 6 strings - Only 5 sound

D/C

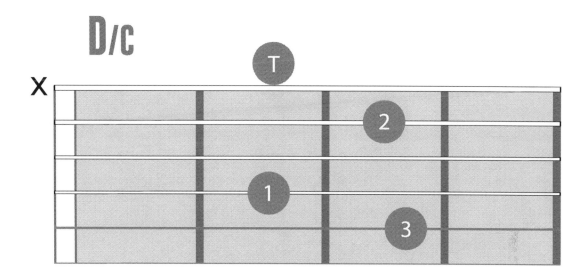

- Thumb touching 6th string
- 3rd finger in middle of fret
- Strum 6 strings - Only 5 sound

Dsus2

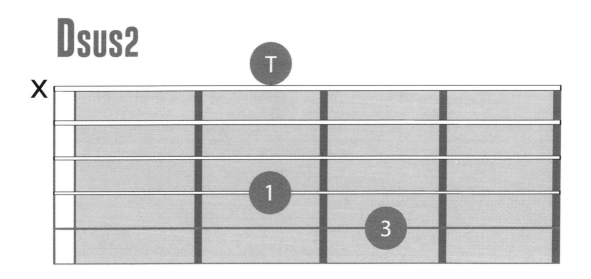

- Thumb touching 6th string
- 3rd finger in middle of fret
- Strum 6 strings - Only 5 sound

Dsus2 *Another Way*

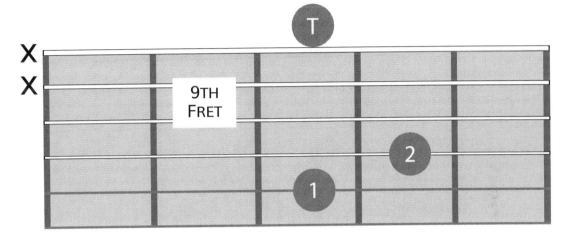

- Thumb touching 6th string
- 1st finger in corner of fret
- Strum bottom 4 strings

Dsus4

- Thumb touching 6th string
- 3rd finger in middle of fret
- Strum 6 strings - Only 5 sound

D5

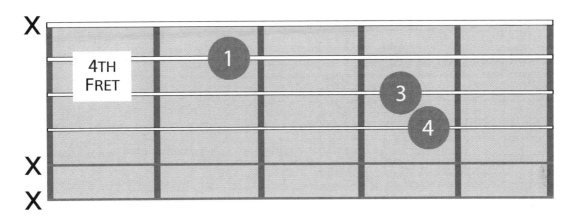

- Thumb low and centred
- 1st finger touching 6th string
- Strum 5th 4th and 3rd strings

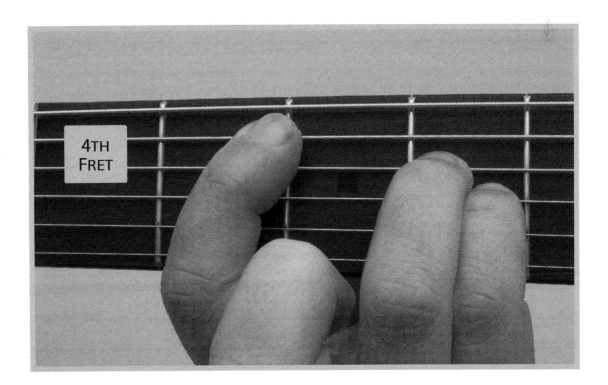

D6

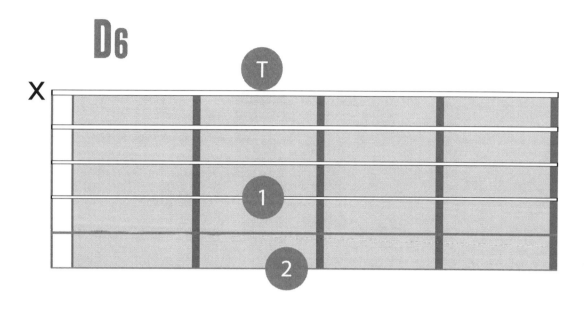

- Thumb touching 6th string
- Can also be played with 2nd and 3rd finger
- Strum 6 strings - Only 5 sound

D6/9

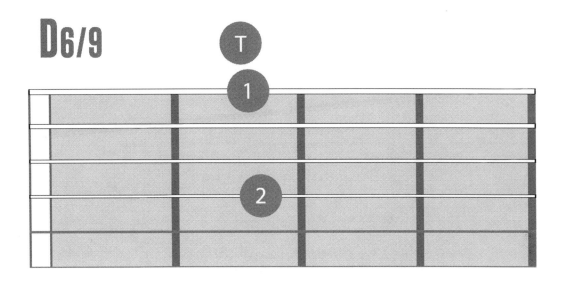

- 5th string muted by inside of 1st finger
- Can also be played with 2nd and 3rd finger
- Strum 6 strings - Only 5 sound

D7

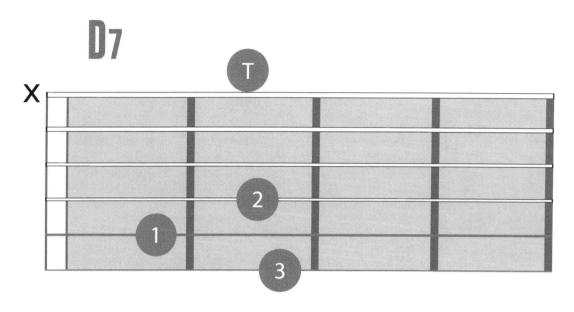

- Thumb touching 6th string
- 1st finger in corner of fret
- Strum 6 strings - Only 5 sound

D7 *ANOTHER WAY*

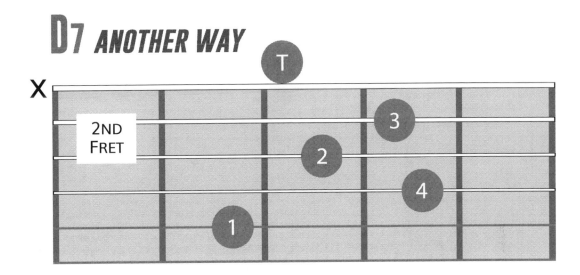

- Thumb touching 6th string
- 1st finger in corner of fret
- Strum 6 strings - Only 5 sound

Dm7

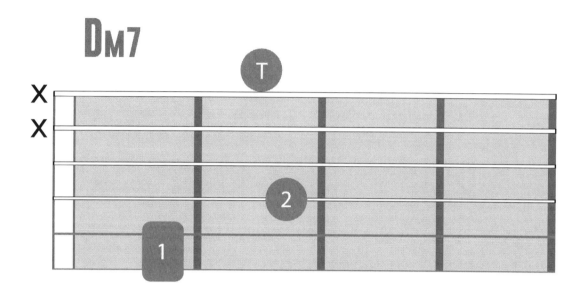

- Grab the guitar neck
- 1st finger pressing 2 strings
- Strum bottom 4 strings

DM7 *ANOTHER WAY*

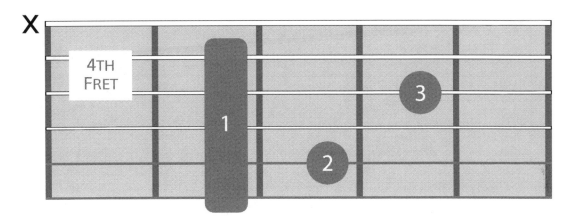

- Thumb low and centred
- 1st finger touching 6th string
- Strum 6 strings - Only 5 sound

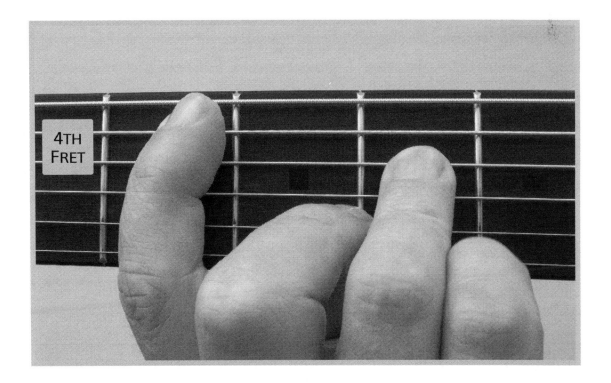

DMAJ7

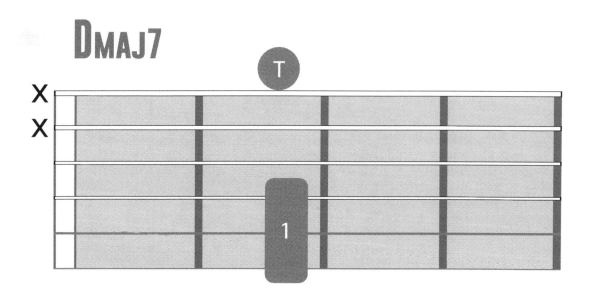

- Sometimes played instead of D
- 1st finger pressing 3 strings
- Strum bottom 4 strings

DMAJ9

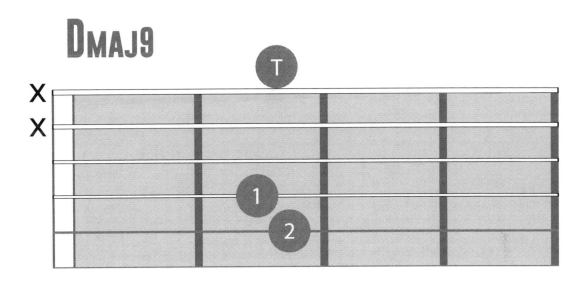

- Thumb touching 6th string
- Can also be played with 2nd & 3rd fingers
- Strum bottom 4 strings

D/E

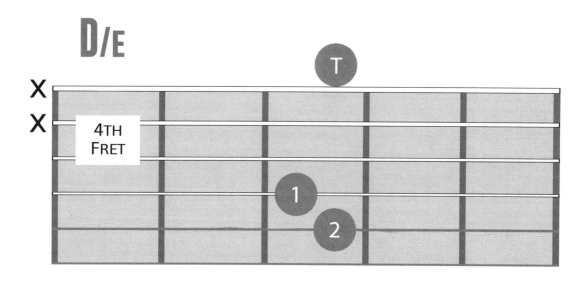

- Thumb touching 6th string
- Can also be played with 2nd & 3rd fingers
- Strum bottom 4 strings

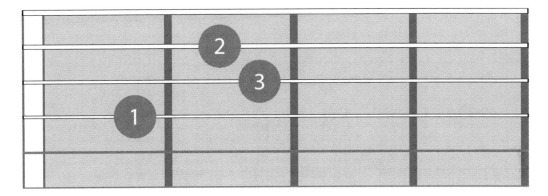

- Thumb not touching 6th string
- 1st finger in corner of fret
- All 6 strings sound

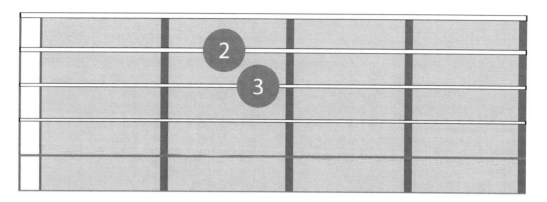

- Thumb not touching 6th string
- Can also be played with 1st and 2nd finger
- All 6 strings sound

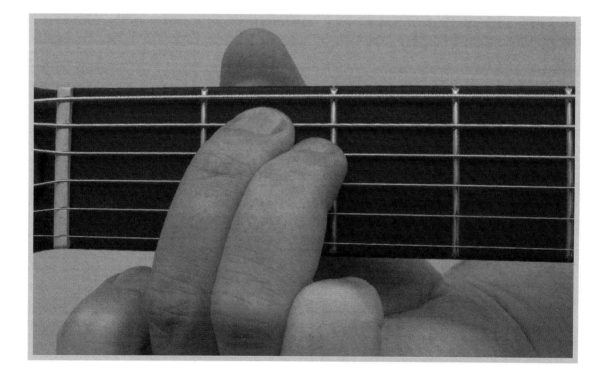

EM *ANOTHER WAY*

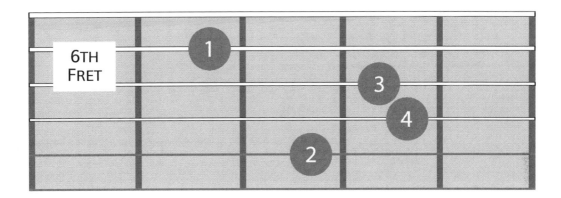

- Thumb low and centred
- 1st finger not touching 6th string
- All 6 strings sound

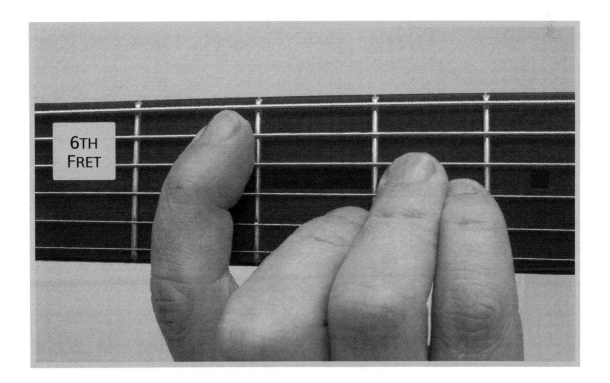

Esus4

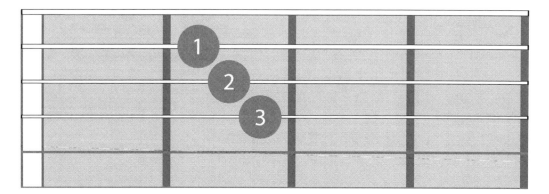

- Thumb not touching 6th string
- Can also be played with 2nd 3rd and 4th finger
- All 6 strings sound

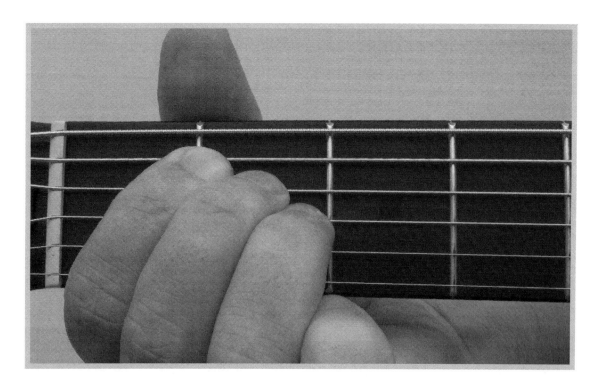

E7sus4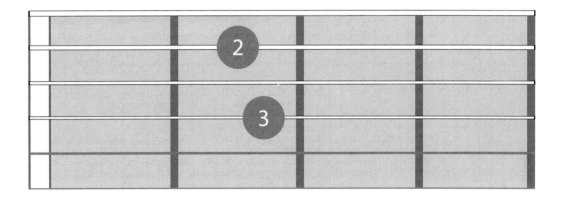

- Thumb not touching 6th string
- Can also be played with 1st and 2nd finger
- All 6 strings sound

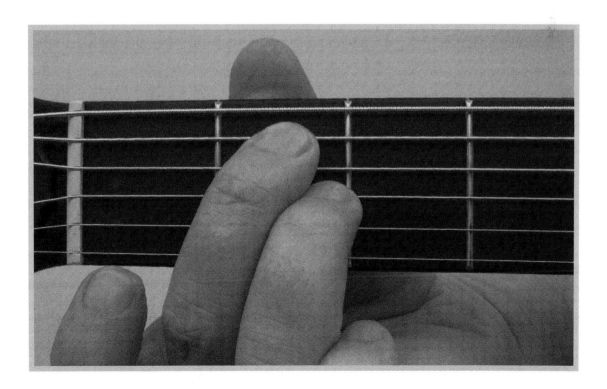

E5

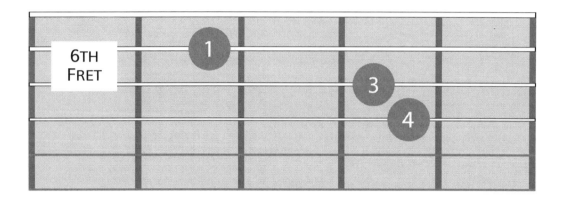

6TH
FRET

- Thumb low and centred
- 1st finger not touching 6th string
- All 6 strings sound

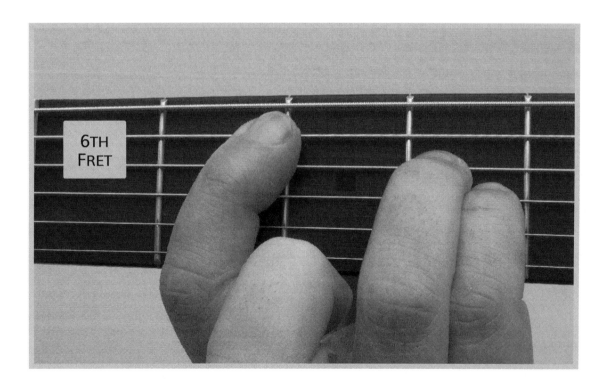

6TH
FRET

Emaj7

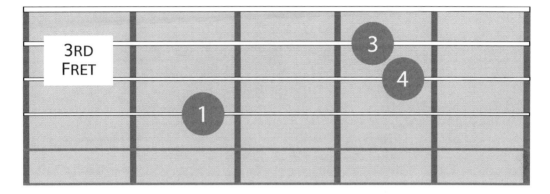

3RD FRET

- Sometimes played instead of E
- Thumb not touching 6th string
- All 6 strings sound

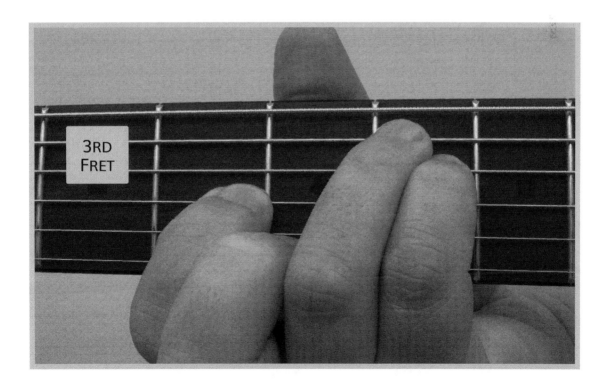

3RD FRET

E7

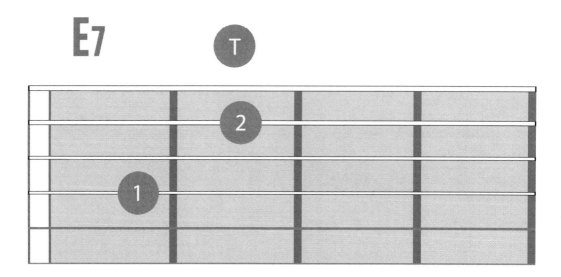

- Thumb not touching 6th string
- 1st finger in corner of fret
- All 6 strings sound

E7 ANOTHER WAY

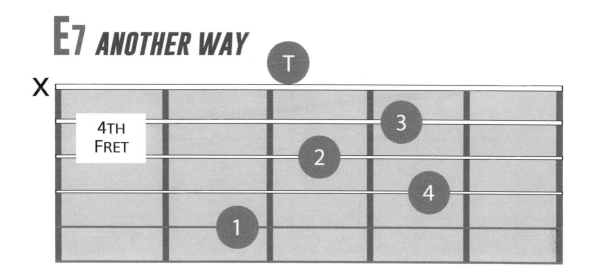

- Thumb touching 6th string
- 1st finger in corner of fret
- All 6 strings sound

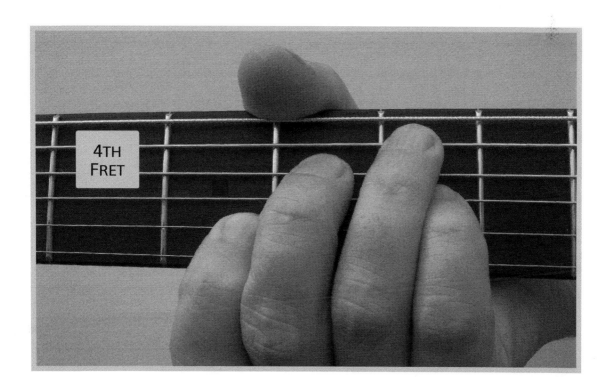

Em7

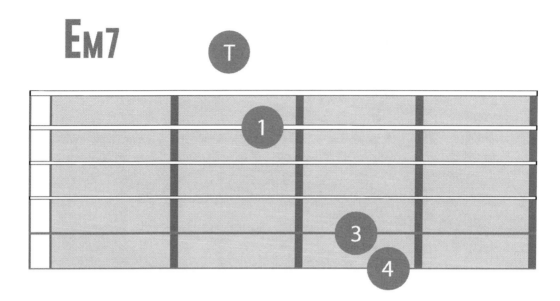

- Thumb not touching 6th string
- 4th string muted by inside of 2nd finger
- Strum 6 strings - Only 5 sound

EM7 *EASIER*

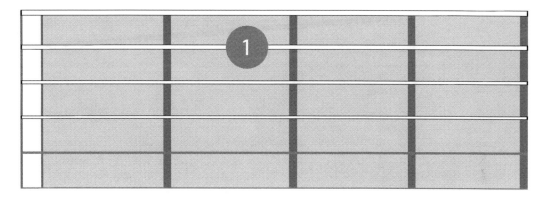

- Thumb not touching 6th string
- Also played with 2nd finger
- All 6 strings sound

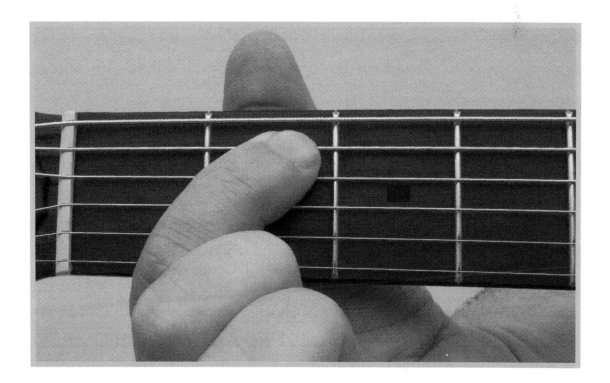

Em/g

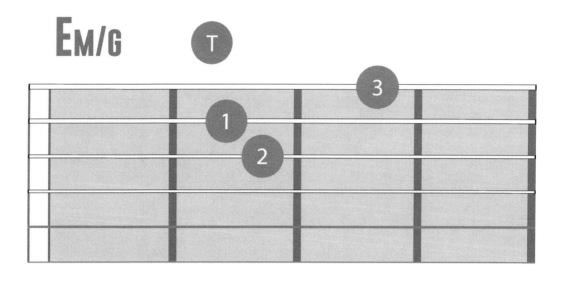

- Thumb may or may not touch 6th string
- Can also be played with 2nd 3rd and 4th finger
- All 6 strings sound

EM11

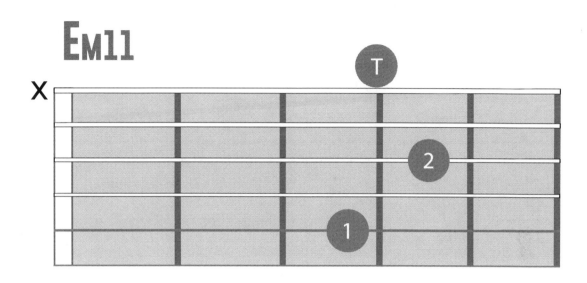

- Sometimes played instead of Em
- Thumb touching 6th string
- Strum 6 strings - Only 5 sound

2ND FRET

F

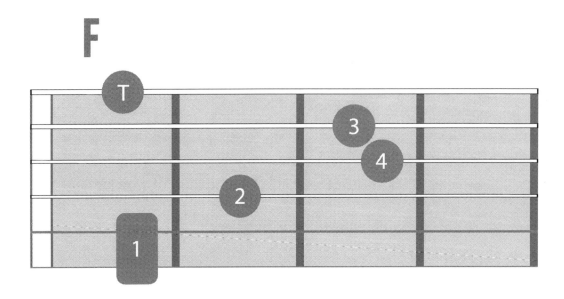

- Grab the guitar neck
- Thumb pressing 6th string
- All 6 strings sound

F *EASIER*

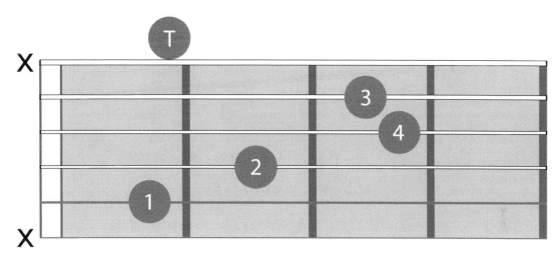

- Grab the guitar neck
- Thumb touching 6th string
- Strum 6 strings - Only 4 sound

F *BARRE CHORD*

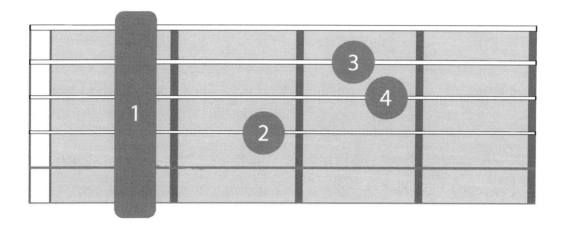

- Thumb low and centred
- Thumb pressing 6th string
- All 6 strings sound

Fм

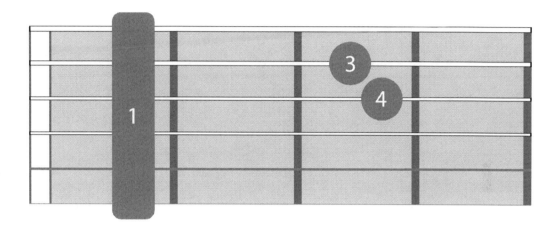

- Stretch your hand
- Thumb low and centred
- All 6 strings sound

Fsus2

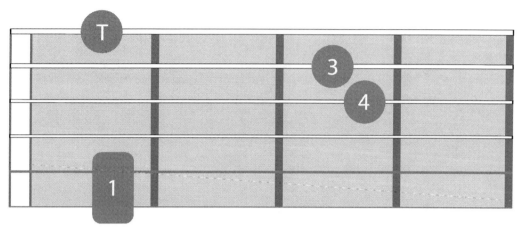

- Grab the guitar neck
- Thumb pressing 6th string
- All 6 strings sound

F5

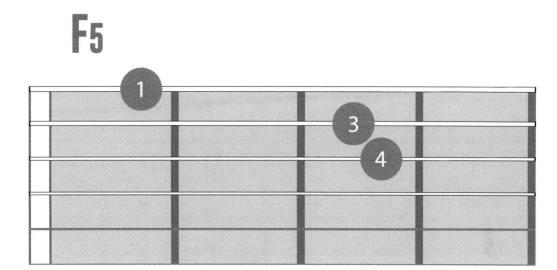

- Stretch your hand
- Thumb low and centred
- Strum 6th 5th and 4th strings

F6

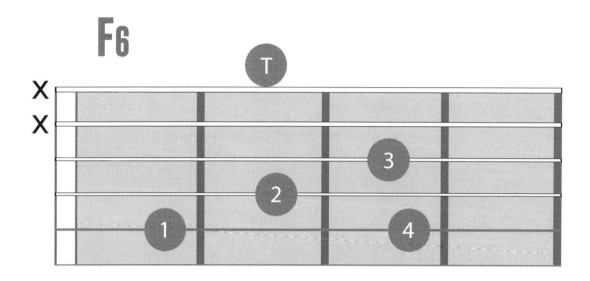

- Thumb touching 6th string
- 1st finger also on 2nd string
  (makes chord changing easier)
- Strum bottom 4 strings

F<small>M</small>7

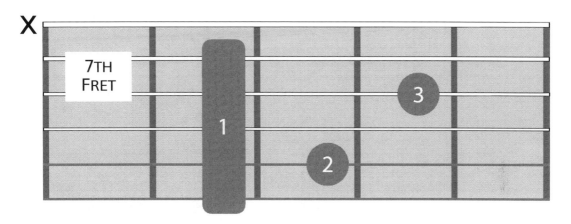

- Thumb low and centred
- 1st finger touching 6th string
- Strum 6 strings - Only 5 sound

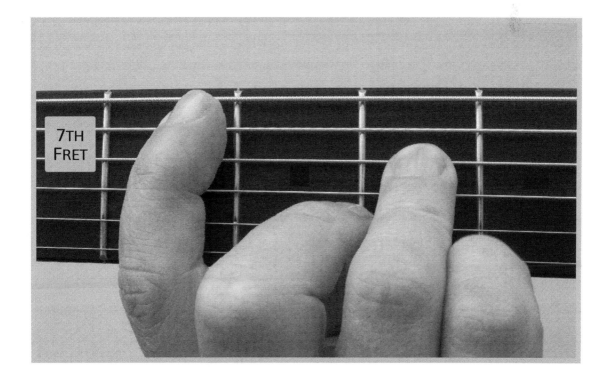

Fmaj7

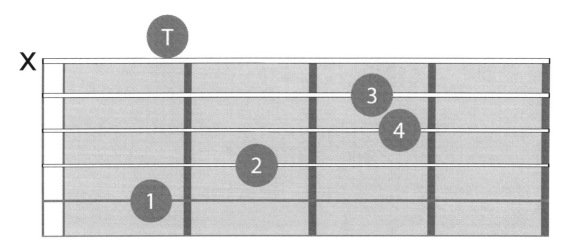

- Grab the guitar neck
- Thumb touching 6th string
- Strum 6 strings - Only 5 sound

FMAJ7 *EASIER*

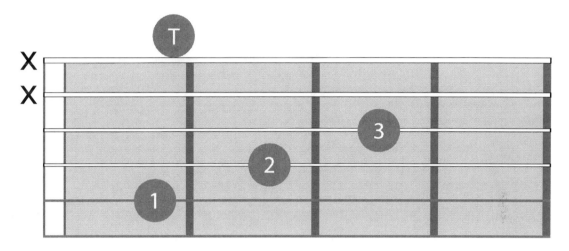

- Sometimes played instead of F
- Thumb touching 6th string
- Strum bottom 4 strings

FMAJ7 *ANOTHER WAY*

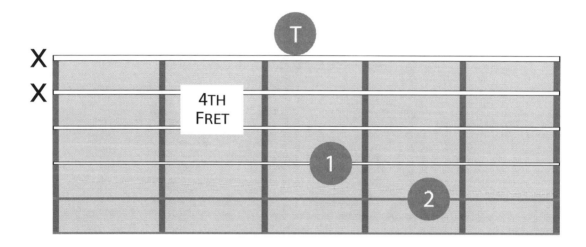

- Thumb touching 6th string
- Can also be played with 1st and 2nd finger
- Strum bottom 4 strings

F#

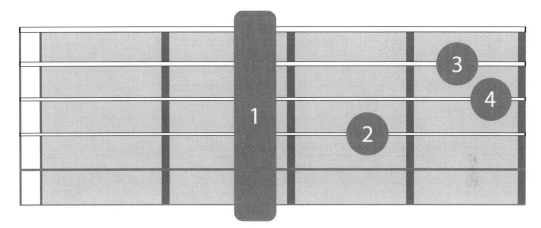

- Stretch your hand
- Thumb low and centred
- All 6 strings sound

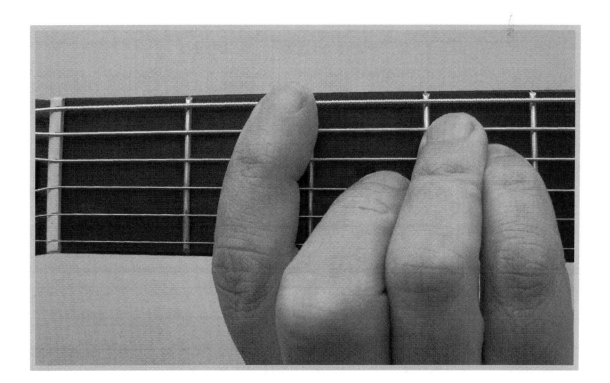

F#m

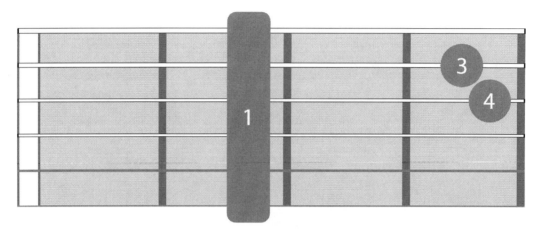

- Stretch your hand
- Thumb low and centred
- All 6 strings sound

F#M *EASIER*

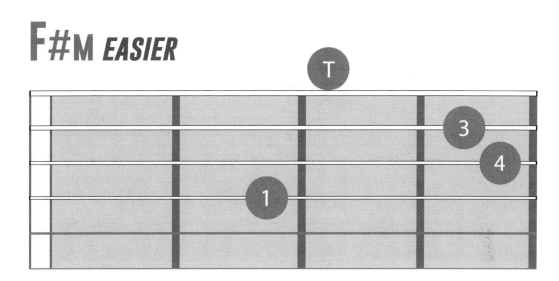

- Grab the guitar neck
- Thumb touching 6th string
- Strum 6 strings - Only 5 sound

F#M7

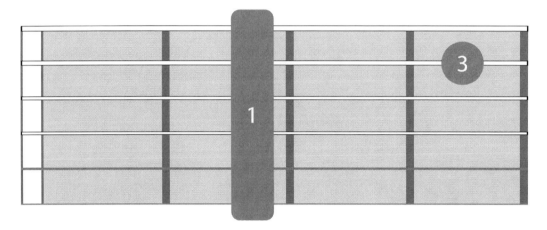

- Stretch your hand
- Thumb low and centred
- All 6 strings sound

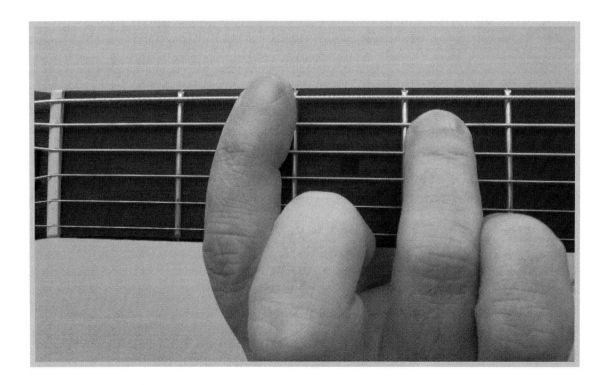

F#M7 *EASIER*

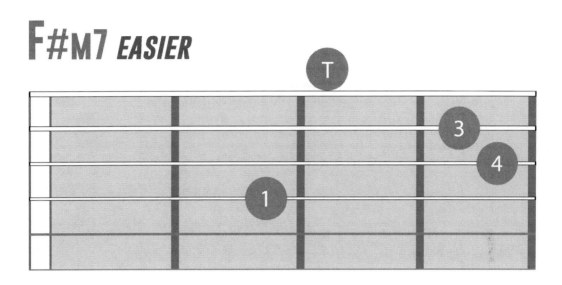

- Grab the guitar neck
- Thumb touching 6th string
- Strum 6 strings - Only 5 sound

F#7

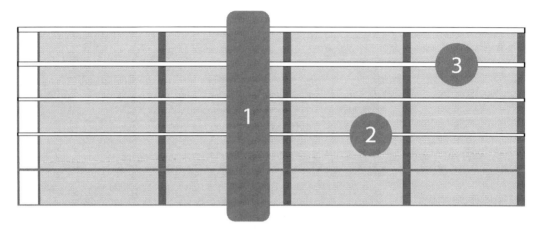

- Stretch your hand
- Thumb low and centred
- All 6 strings sound

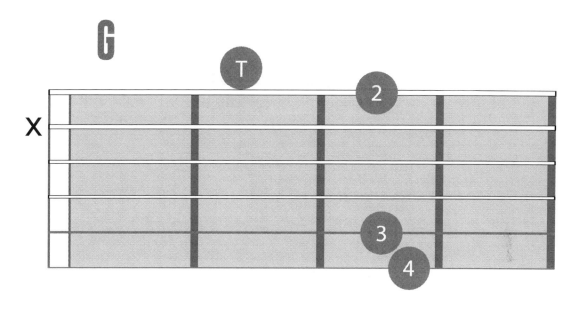

G

- Thumb may or may not touch 6th string
- 5th string muted by inside of 2nd finger
- Strum 6 strings - Only 5 sound

G *EASIER*

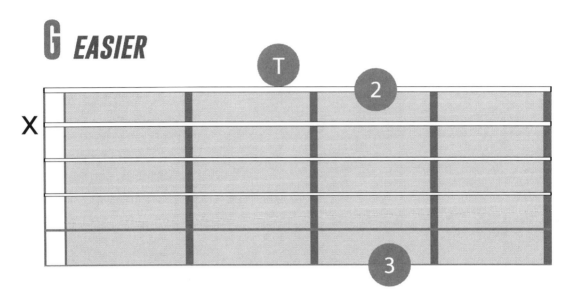

- Thumb can touch 6th string
- 5th string muted by inside of 2nd finger
- Strum 6 strings - Only 5 sound

G ANOTHER WAY

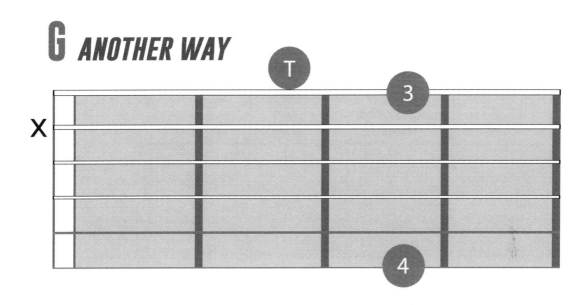

- Thumb may or may not touch 6th string
- 5th string muted by inside of 3rd finger
- Strum 6 strings - Only 5 sound

Gm

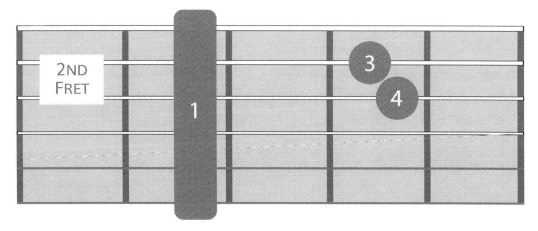

- Stretch your hand
- Thumb low and centred
- All 6 strings sound

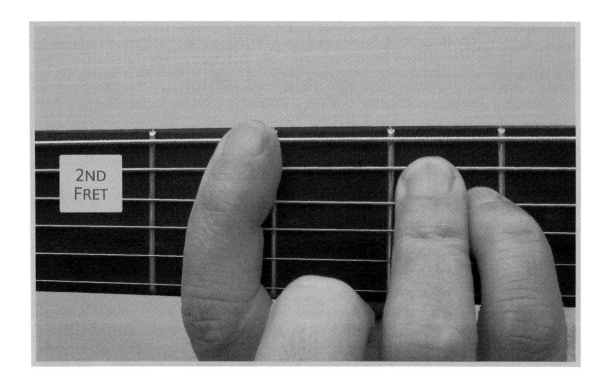

G/F#

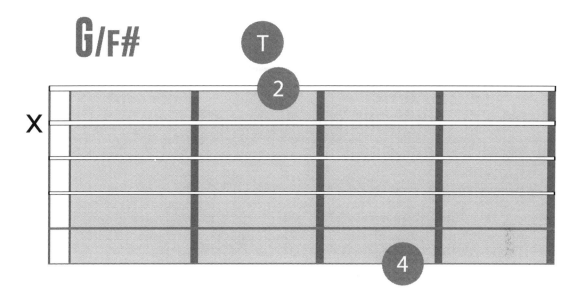

- Thumb may or may not touch 6th string
- 5th string muted by inside of 2nd finger
- Strum 6 strings - Only 5 sound

G/B

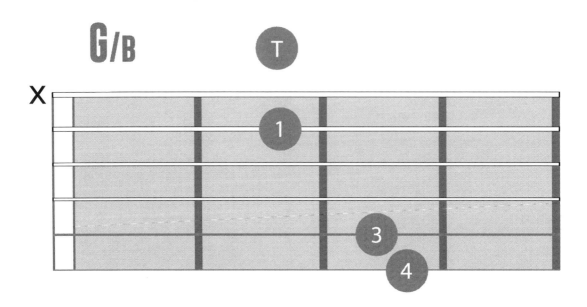

- Thumb may or may not touch 6th string
- 6th string does not sound
- Strum bottom 5 strings only

G/c

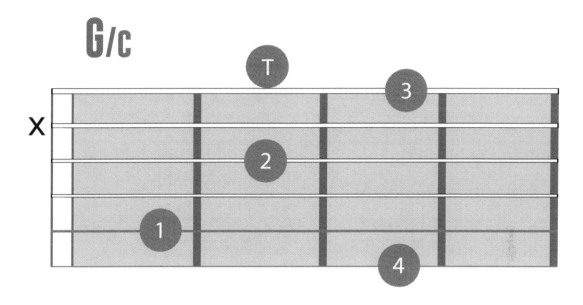

- Thumb may or may not touch 6th string
- 5th string muted by inside of 3rd finger
- Strum 6 strings - Only 5 sound

Gsus4

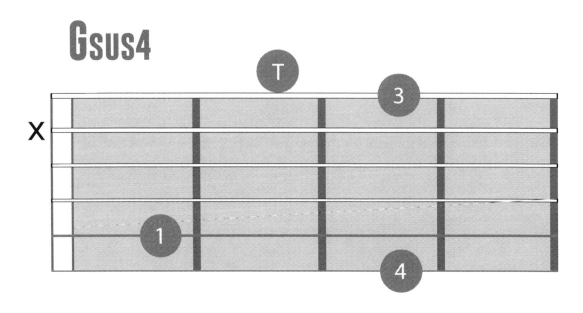

- Thumb may or may not touch 6th string
- 5th string muted by inside of 3rd finger
- Strum 6 strings - Only 5 sound

G5

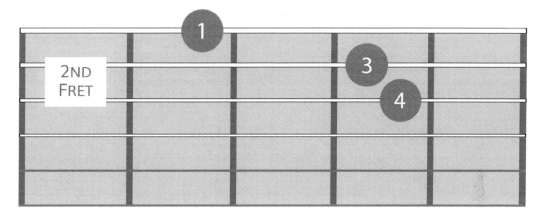

- Stretch your hand
- Thumb low and centred
- Strum 6th 5th and 4th strings

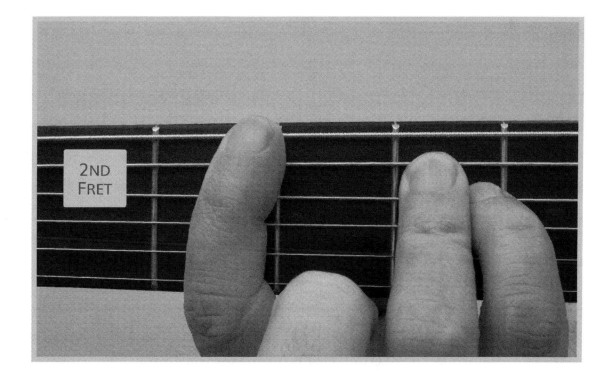

G6

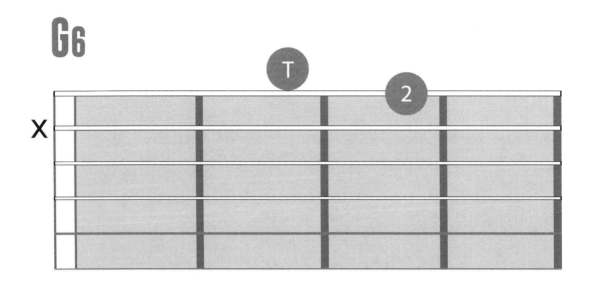

- Thumb may or may not touch 6th string
- 5th string muted by inside of 2nd finger
- Strum 6 strings - Only 5 sound

G7

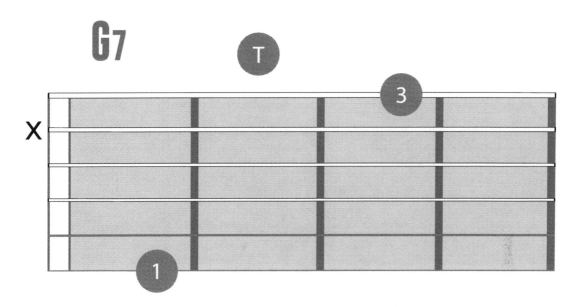

- Thumb may or may not touch 6th string
- 5th string muted by inside of 3rd finger
- Strum 6 strings - Only 5 sound

GMAJ7

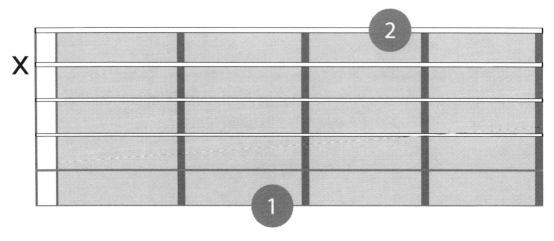

X

- 5th string muted by inside of 2nd finger
- Can also be played with 2nd and 3rd finger
- Strum 6 strings - Only 5 sound

GMAJ7 *EASIER*

- Thumb may or may not touch 6th string
- Can also be played with 2nd finger
- Strum bottom 4 strings

Gmaj7 *another way*

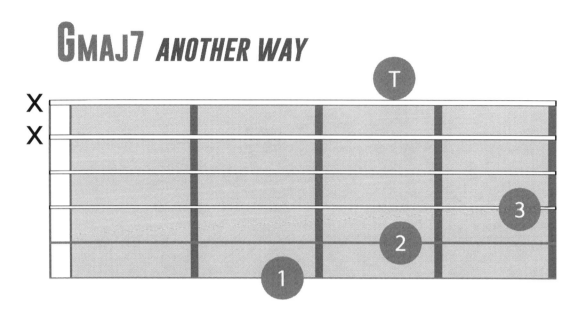

- Sometimes played instead of G
- Thumb touching 6th string
- Strum bottom 4 strings

Gm7

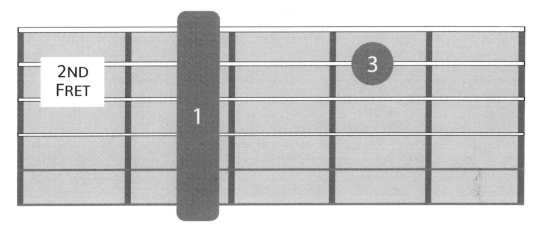

2ND
FRET

- Stretch your hand
- Thumb low and centred
- All 6 strings sound

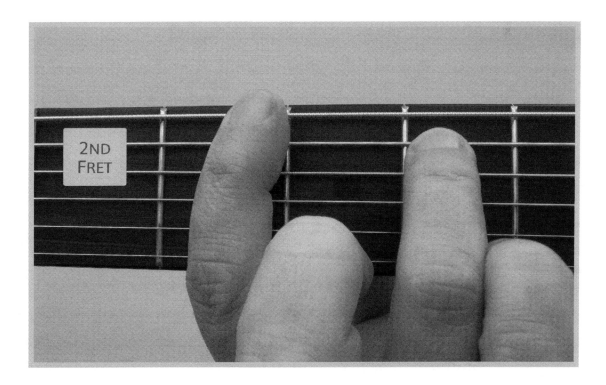

2ND
FRET

G/D7

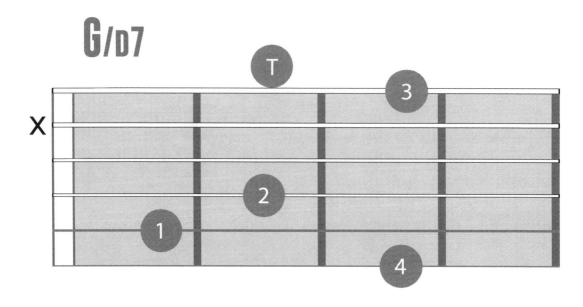

- Thumb may or may not touch 6th string
- 5th string muted by inside of 3rd finger
- Strum 6 strings - Only 5 sound

G/A

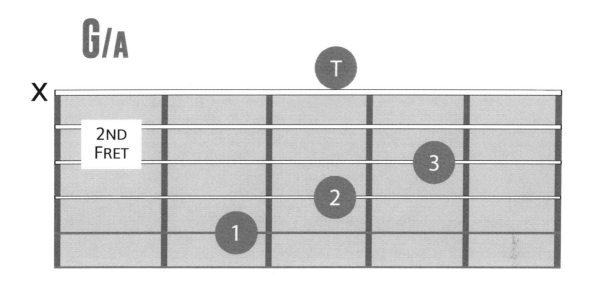

- Sometimes played instead of G
- Thumb touching 6th string
- Strum 6 strings - Only 5 sound

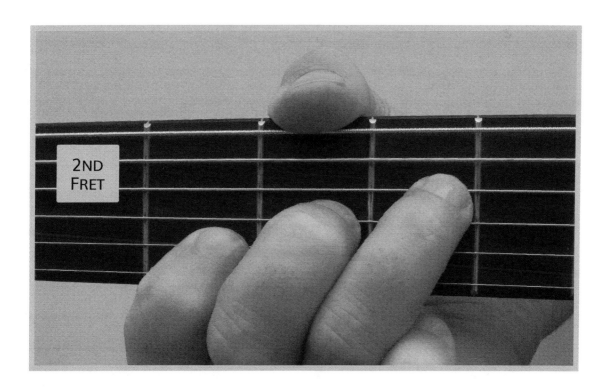

Gadd9

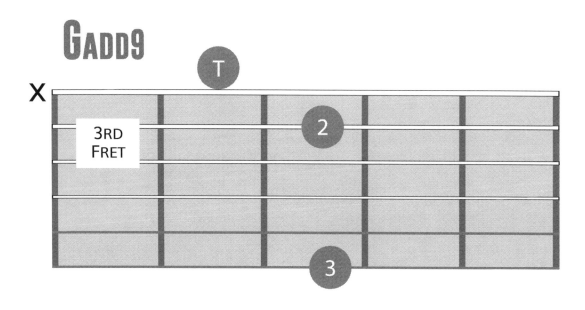

- Sometimes played instead of G
- Thumb touching 6th string
- Strum 6 strings - Only 5 sound

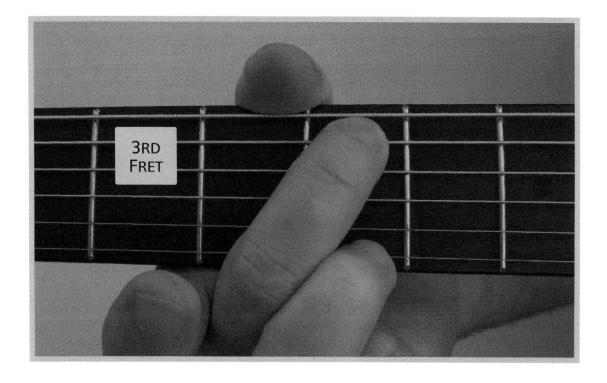

G#

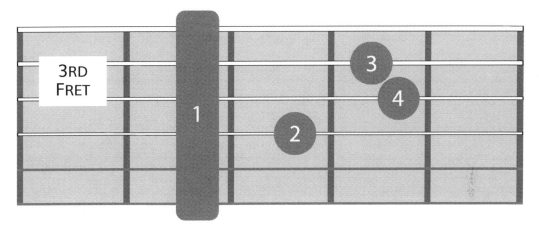

3RD FRET

- Stretch your hand
- Thumb low and centred
- All 6 strings sound

3RD FRET

NOTES

Questions or Thoughts

Email

support@pauricmather.com

I would love to hear from you.

Review Request

If you have a moment, please leave a review. Your feedback greatly helps all of us on our musical journey.

MEET THE AUTHOR

Pauric Mather's ground breaking guitar books and lessons are truly unique. Easily the most individual and personalised you will ever find. They have helped thousands of people to learn guitar. What's even more remarkable is that you need no knowledge of music to learn from his teaching style.

As well as being an expert guitar teacher, Pauric Mather is the author of 4 #1 best sellers.

From Dublin, Ireland, he's been a professional guitarist since 1987, and has worked with many successful artists.

Pauric Mather is now the most translated guitar author in the world. His books and teaching methods are available in more than 10 languages.

LIVE WEBINAR - VIDEO - EMAIL SUPPORT

For all students learning from Pauric Mather guitar books.
Ask questions about anything you need help with.

Email support@pauricmather.com

Also By The Author

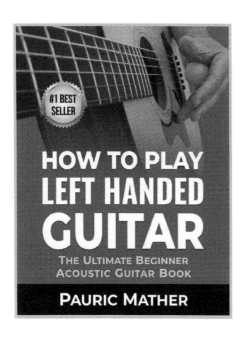 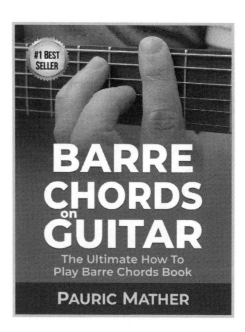

Available in other languages

Made in the USA
Las Vegas, NV
28 November 2023

81674179R00072